SWEDEN
the land

April Fast and Keltie Thomas

A Bobbie Kalman Book

The Lands, Peoples, and Cultures Series

Crabtree Publishing Company

www.crabtreebooks.com

The Lands, Peoples, and Cultures Series

Created by Bobbie Kalman

Coordinating editor
Ellen Rodger

Project editor
Sean Charlebois

Production coordinator
Rosie Gowsell

Project development, design, editing, and photo research
First Folio Resource Group, Inc.
   Erinn Banting
   Molly Bennett
   Tom Dart
   Alana Lai
   Jaimie Nathan
   Debbie Smith
   Anikó Szocs

Prepress and printing
Worzalla Publishing Company

Consultant
Marita Karlisch, Archivist/Librarian,
American Swedish Institute

Photographs
AFP/Corbis/Magma: p. 27 (bottom); B & C Alexander/
Photo Researchers: p. 30 (top); Ellen Barone/Houserstock:
p. 15 (right); Mikael Bertmar/Tiofoto: p. 20; Jonathan
Blair/Corbis/Magma: p. 24 (bottom); Tibor Bognàr: p. 16
(right); Scott Camazine/Photo Researchers: p. 28 (left); John
Corbett/Ecoscene/ Corbis/Magma: p. 4; Macduff
Everton/Corbis/Magma: p. 8 (bottom), p. 11 (top), p. 16 (left),
p. 17 (top), p. 18 (left); Michael Freeman/Corbis/Magma: p. 25
(left); Francois Gohier/Photo Researchers: p. 31 (bottom);
Farrell Grehan/Photo Researchers: p. 7 (right); Lars Guvå High
Coast World Heritage Site: p. 9 (bottom); Hal Horwitz/
Corbis/Magma: p. 3; Len Kaufman: p. 17 (bottom); Jan-Peter
Lahall/Peter Arnold: p. 7 (left), p. 8 (top), p. 9 (top), p. 13, p. 21
(bottom), p. 22 (left), p. 23; Charles & Josette Lenars/Corbis/
Magma: p. 5 (top); Chris Lisle/Corbis/Magma: p. 10, p. 19;
Tom McHugh/Photo Researchers: p. 30 (bottom); John
Noble/Corbis/Magma: p. 6, p. 26; Rolf Nyström/Tiofoto: p. 25
(right); Pekka Parviainen/Science Photo Library/Photo
Researchers: p. 12; Ted Spiegel/Corbis/Magma: p. 15 (left);
Hans Strand/ Corbis/Magma: p. 11 (bottom); Roger Tidman/
Corbis/ Magma: p. 28 (right), p. 29 (top); Trip/F. Austin: p. 27
(top); Trip/M. Fairman: p. 22 (right); Trip/C. Rennie: title
page, p. 5 (bottom); Trip/A. Tovy: p. 18 (right); Robert van der
Hilst/Corbis/Magma: p. 21 (top); Hans Strand/Getty
Images/Image Bank (cover); Dan Vander Zwalm/Corbis/
Magma: p. 24 (top); Staffan Widstrand/Corbis/ Magma: p. 29
(bottom); Winfried Wisniewsky/Photo Researchers: p. 31 (top);
Bo Zaunders/Corbis/Magma: p. 14

Every effort has been made to obtain the appropriate credit
and full copyright clearance for all images in this book. Any
oversights, despite Crabtree's greatest precautions, will be
corrected in future editions.

Map
Jim Chernishenko

Illustrations
Dianne Eastman: icon
David Wysotski, Allure Illustrations: back cover

Cover: The winter sun rises over packed snow and ice on the
Gulf of Bothnia between Sweden and Finland.

Icon: The Scots pine, which appears at head of each section
grows well in Sweden's far north where the land is frozen for
seven or eight months each year.

Title page: Modern and ancient buildings crowd the island of
Stadsholmen, which is part of Stockholm. Stadsholmen is one
of the fourteen islands that make up Sweden's capital city.

Back cover: Herring, silvery fish that grow to be 10 inches
(25 centimeters) long, swim in large schools in the Baltic Sea,
off the eastern coast of Sweden.

Note: When using foreign terms, the author has followed the
Swedish style of only capitalizing people and place names.

Published by
Crabtree Publishing Company

PMB 16A,	612 Welland Avenue	73 Lime Walk
350 Fifth Avenue	St. Catharines	Headington
Suite 3308	Ontario, Canada	Oxford OX3 7AD
New York	L2M 5V6	United Kingdom
N.Y. 10118		

Thomas, Keltie, 1966-
  Sweden : the land / Keltie Thomas.
     p. cm. -- (Lands, peoples, and cultures series)
"A Bobbie Kalman Book."
Includes index.
Summary: Describes the geography, climate, history, cities,
agriculture, transportation, business and trade, and wildlife
of Sweden.
  ISBN 0-7787-9327-3 (rlb) -- ISBN 0-7787-9695-7 (pbk.)
  1. Sweden--Description and travel--Juvenile literature. [1.
Sweden--Description and travel.] I. Title. II. Series.
  DL619.T494 2004
  914.85--dc22
                          2003016422
                             LC

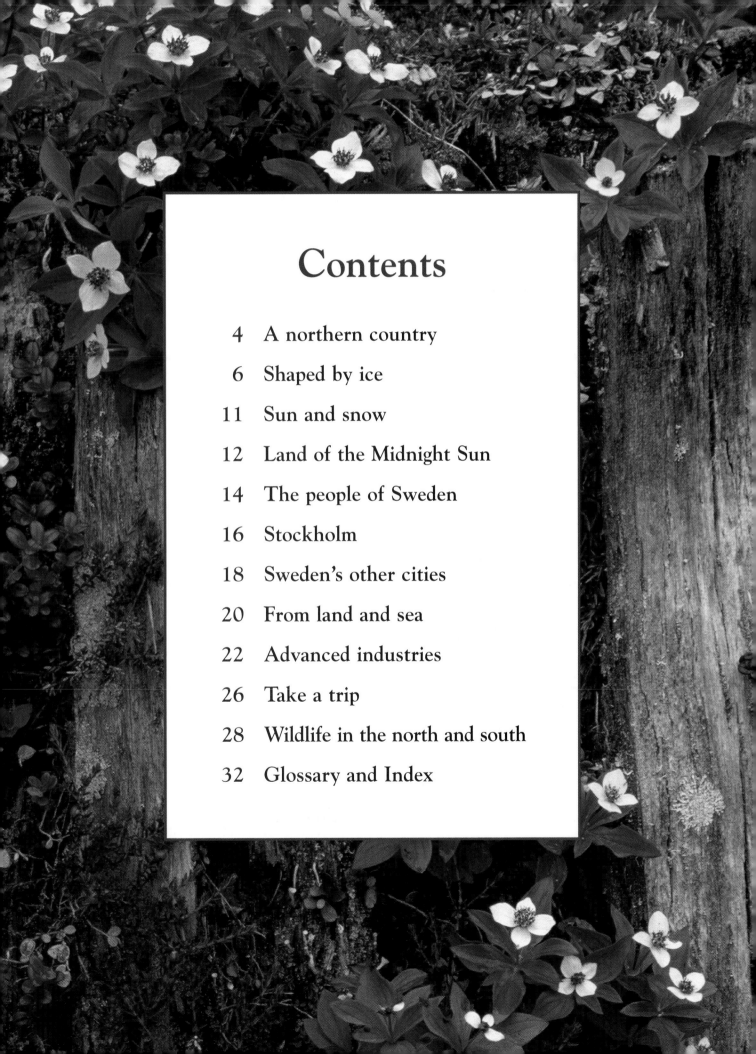

Contents

 A northern country

The Scandinavian Peninsula, in northern Europe, is shared by two countries — Sweden and its western neighbor, Norway. Sweden is a long, narrow country shaped like a crooked finger. It is bordered by the Baltic Sea and Gulf of Bothnia, which lap along its eastern coast, the Skagerrak and Kattegat Seas, in the southwest, and the Öresund Strait, which separates Sweden from Denmark, a country to the south.

A varied land

Snow-capped mountains and **glaciers** cover Sweden's far north, which is close to the freezing North Pole. They give way to dense forests and **fertile** plains in the south, and sandy beaches and rocky shores along the coasts.

(top) In Jovattnet, a village in the far north, people live in red and white cottages called stugas. The people in the village grow crops, such as potatoes, and fish in nearby lakes for fresh salmon.

Most Swedes live in cities or villages in the south, where they manufacture computers and **pharmaceuticals**, work in the **pulp** and paper industry, or grow crops such as wheat and barley. Of the few Swedes who live in the far north, most are Sami, one of the country's first peoples. Many Sami farm and herd reindeer, some of which roam wild with moose, bears, lemmings, and foxes.

Facts at a glance

Official name: Kingdom of Sweden (Kungariket Sverige)
Area: 158,620 square miles (410,934 square kilometers)
Population: 8,876,744
Capital city: Stockholm
Official language: Swedish
Main religion: Lutheran
Currency: Swedish krona
National holiday: Flag Day (June 6)

Factories, warehouses, and ships loaded with cargo crowd Stockholm's main port. Stockholm, in the east, is Sweden's capital and the country's center of trade and industry.

A cyclist locks her bike outside a café in Göteborg, on the western coast. Many Swedes use bicycles to travel through busy city streets.

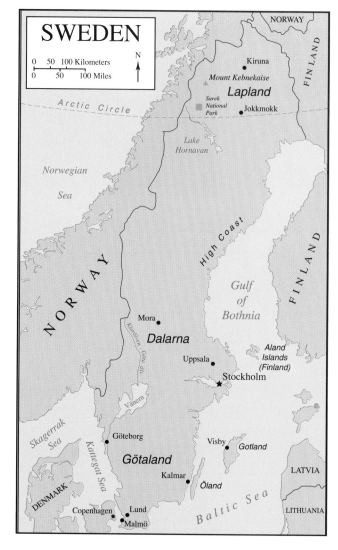

(left) Dogsledders travel through the icy Kebnekaise National Park, in the north. Glaciers in the park have been slowly melting for tens of thousands of years.

Fourteen thousand years ago, an enormous glacier blanketed all of Europe, including Sweden, and parts of Asia. The weight of the ice pushed Sweden below the sea. When the ice melted 10,000 years ago, the land began to rise back to its original height. Parts of eastern Sweden are still rising to this day.

The melting ice moved over Sweden and changed its landscape. It rounded mountains, carved out valleys and lakes, formed sandy ridges and hollows, and deposited rich soil in the south.

Mountain ranges

The Kölen Mountains stretch from north to south along Sweden's border with Norway. The highest peak, Kebnekaise, or Mount Kebne, towers 6,926 feet (2,111 meters) above the frozen, rocky landscape in the far north. The mountains in the far north are jagged, treeless, and capped by glaciers. Few roads or paths run through them, and those that do are dangerous because of avalanches caused by the continuously melting glaciers. Forests, villages, and farms crop up in green valleys that cling to the sides of mountains in the south.

(above) A brook rushes through moss-covered mountains in Sarek National Park, in northeastern Sweden. The weight of the glaciers in this area was so great that many mountain peaks became completely rounded.

Dense forests

Coniferous trees, such as Scots pine and Norwegian spruce, grow in the large forested area that extends from the mountains in the north through central Sweden. These trees, which bear cones, are able to survive in colder climates. Forests in the warmer south are filled with deciduous trees, such as birch, ash, maple, and elm. Unlike coniferous trees, deciduous trees shed their leaves in the winter.

(right) Deciduous forests in the south turn vibrant shades of yellow, red, and orange in the fall.

Farms stretch across the plains in Skåne, a region in the south.

Southern lands

Southern Sweden is dominated by lowlands, which are broad areas of flat land dotted with lakes, forests, and farmland. In the middle of the lowlands is the Götaland Plateau, or Swedish Highlands. Scientists believe the **limestone** plateau was once part of the Kölen mountain range, but was worn almost completely flat by glaciers.

Winding rivers

Rivers that begin in the mountains wind their way through the valleys and plains in the rest of Sweden. Some rivers empty into lakes, and others reach all the way to the coasts. Rivers are used to transport goods, irrigate, or water, farmers' fields, and power homes and factories. The longest river is the Klarälven-Göta. During its 447-mile (720-kilometer) journey from the Kölen Mountains to the Kattegat Sea, the Klarälven-Göta rushes through dark forests, open fields, and cities, such as Göteborg.

Deep lakes

There are more than 100,000 lakes in Sweden. When the glaciers tore across the land, they ripped up large chunks of rock and washed away soil, leaving large, empty basins that eventually filled with water. Sweden has some of the deepest lakes in the world. The deepest lake is Lake Hornavan, in the north. It plunges 725 feet (221 meters) below ground. That is equivalent to two and a quarter soccer fields.

Kiruna, a town in the north, stands on Kaalasjarvi Lake. The majority of Sweden's lakes are in the north.

Mist rises from a peat bog in the south. Some peat bogs are drained so large strips of peat can be harvested.

The High Coast has risen nearly 300 feet (91 meters) since the last Ice Age ended nearly 10,000 years ago. Scientists predict that the coast will rise another 164 feet (50 meters) over the next 10,000 years.

Peat bogs

Some of Sweden's shallow lakes are now peat bogs. Peat bogs form when lakes in lowland areas fill up with mud, plants, and mosses that decompose, or break down, over time. Swedes harvest the decomposed material, which is called peat. It is mixed with soil and used to **fertilize** crops and gardens, or burned to heat and power factories.

On the coasts

Sweden's 2,000-mile- (3,218-kilometer-) long coast has rocky shores in the southwest, sandy beaches in the south, and steep cliffs in the east. Höga Kusten, or the High Coast, in the northeast, is still rising out of the water. This produces rich soil in the area that is found nowhere else in the north. The soil allows some species of deciduous trees, such as hazel and maple, and wildflowers, such as the purple saxifrage, to grow despite the northern climate.

Skärgården

Off the coast of Stockholm is Skärgården, or the Stockholm Archipelago. It is made up of more than 24,000 small islands. Some are so small that people can walk from end to end in less than an hour. Many are covered in forests and meadows, and others, called skerries, are bare and rocky.

Cottages are built on many of the islands in Skärgården. People live there all year or vacation there during the summer. During the winter, when the Baltic Sea freezes, residents of islands close to the coast sometimes hike, ski, or snowshoe to the mainland.

(top) A limestone pillar, or raukar, *stands at the edge of the island of Gotland, off Sweden's eastern coast. According to legend, one of Gotland's* raukar, *called Hoburgsgubben, is really a mean troll who was turned to stone by a brave man named Tor.*

Gotland and Öland

The large islands of Gotland and Öland lie in the Baltic Sea. According to legend, Gotland was once placed under a spell that made it sink into the sea every evening and rise out of the sea every morning. To break the spell, a man named Tjelvar brought fire to the island. The fire lit up the night sky and made it seem as if it were always day. The island never sank again. Although most people do not believe this legend, there is evidence that thousands of years ago Gotland was submerged by the sea many times.

Gotland and Öland are made of sandstone and limestone. Tall pillars of limestone, called *raukar*, stand along the islands' coasts. The *raukar* were created when wind and waves eroded, or wore away, the rock. In the fine sand that covers the islands' beaches, orchids and other rare flowers grow. These flowers are found nowhere else in Sweden.

Sun and snow

The weather in Sweden varies as much as its landscape. Winters in the south last two or three months, and temperatures average 32° Fahrenheit (0° Celsius). Summer temperatures average 70° Fahrenheit (22° Celsius) and it is often rainy. In the north, winters last seven to eight months and temperatures average 10° Fahrenheit (–12° Celsius), but can drop to –40° Fahrenheit (–40° Celsius). Northern summers are only a few months long. On the hottest days, temperatures only reach 54° Fahrenheit (12° Celsius).

The south is warmer than the north because it is far from the North Pole and because of the effects of the Gulf Stream. The Gulf Stream is a swift ocean **current** that carries warm water and wind from the **equator** to Sweden's southern coast.

(right) Sandy beaches line the southern coast of Sweden. People enjoy the sunny weather, swim, and sail in the Baltic Sea during the warm summer months.

(below) Thick snow blankets a storage shed on a farm near Fryksas, a village in the north.

The Northern Lights illuminate the night sky over Kiruna, a city in the north. The best months to see this colorful light show are October, February, and March.

One-seventh of Sweden lies above the Arctic Circle, which is a large area that surrounds the North Pole. The North and South Poles are the points at which Earth tilts on its axis. On the shortest day of the year, December 21, the North Pole tilts the farthest away from the sun, and the sun in the Arctic Circle does not rise.

On the longest day of the year, June 21, the North Pole is closest to the sun, and the sun in the Arctic Circle does not set. For several weeks in June and July, the sun shines almost all night. For this reason, Sweden's far north is often called the Land of the Midnight Sun. People can go outside at midnight to read a book in full daylight!

Northern Lights

On cold, dark winter nights, the sky in the far north is sometimes draped with a glowing veil of dancing colors called the Northern Lights. Scientists call the Northern Lights the aurora borealis, which means "red dawn of the north" in **Latin**. The Northern Lights shimmer across the sky when charged particles from the sun strike gases in the atmosphere surrounding Earth. The collision releases energy, which appears as glowing red, pink, and green lights.

Spring has sprung!

During the north's long winters, the land is buried in up to 80 inches (200 centimeters) of thick, white snow. Snow often piles up as high as the tops of roofs and hydro poles.

When spring finally arrives, it seems that it happens almost overnight. Buds often appear on trees and sprout leaves within one week. All over Sweden, people celebrate spring's arrival on *valborgsmässöafton*, or Walpurgis Eve, which is April 30. This celebration dates from the time of the Vikings, who ruled Sweden between 800 A.D. and 1050 A.D. The Vikings lit bonfires and sang songs on *valborgsmässöafton* to speed up spring's coming and scare off evil spirits. Swedes celebrate *valborgsmässöafton* in the same way today.

(opposite) In summer, water that has melted from glaciers high in the northern mountains feeds rivers that run into fresh lakes. People fish in northern lakes for trout, salmon, and pike.

The people of Sweden

No one is sure where the Sami came from, but **archaeological** evidence shows they have lived in Sweden since 8000 B.C. Between 17,000 and 20,000 Sami live in Sweden today. Sami also live in northern Norway, Finland, and Russia.

The Sami have adapted to the harsh climate in the far north. They survive by hunting and fishing, growing crops during the short summer months, and herding reindeer, which they use for their meat, hides, and milk. The lifestyle of the Sami has been threatened by different settlers and development in Sweden, but their language and many of their customs survive. These customs include singing *joiks*, songs that tell stories about the Sami's past or about people in their lives.

The Sveas and Goths

The **ancestors** of most Swedes are the Sveas and Goths. Scientists think these peoples came from present-day Germany sometime before 100 A.D. and settled in Sweden, Denmark, and Finland. In Sweden, the Sveas settled in the central region, called Svealand, while the Goths settled in the southern area, called Götaland. The powerful Sveas finally overran the Goths, and by 500 A.D., the Sveas had taken over most of the country. Sverige, the Swedish name for Sweden, means "Land of the Sveas."

(top) A Sami family sits outside their traditional wooden home, called a kata. *Sami clothing is often embroided, or decorated, with red, green, yellow, and blue which are the colors of the Sami flag.*

The Vikings

Powerful Svea and Goth chiefs began to explore other countries, such as Russia, to the east. These fierce warriors came to be known as the Vikings. Many Swedes claim Viking ancestry. People still tell stories about the gods and goddesses their ancestors worshiped, such as Thor, the god of thunder, and Freya, the goddess of love. In August, a festival that celebrates Sigurd Fafnirsbane, a brave warrior from Viking folktales, is held near Stockholm. At the festival, **blacksmiths** and jewelers make tools and jewelry in the same style as their Viking ancestors.

A Swedish family takes a walk in the country. In summer, many Swedes have an entire month's vacation. Some people go to the country to enjoy nature, and others visit the cities to see the sights.

Coming to Sweden

Nearly 500,000 Finnish-speaking people live in northeastern Sweden, along the border with Finland. The Finns came to Sweden in three waves: first in the 1500s because of wars in their country, then in the mid-1940s after **World War II** ended, and again in the 1960s, in search of work in the country's rapidly developing manufacturing industry. In the 1960s, workers also arrived from Yugoslavia, Turkey, and Greece. In recent years, people from Bosnia-Herzegovina, Iran, and Iraq have immigrated to escape war and difficult living conditions in their **homelands**. The Swedish government develops many programs that encourage immigrants to keep their culture. For example, Swedish public schools offer classes in as many as 60 languages.

A Swedish girl prepares for a day of cross-country skiing. Sweden's forests, beaches, lakes, and mountains make it an ideal place for outdoor sports and activities.

15

Stockholm

The beginnings of Stockholm

Stockholm grew from a small town settled in 1252 by the Swedish ruler Birger Jarl. Jarl built a castle on Stadsholmen, one of the islands that is now part of Stockholm, where he stored his gold and jewels. By the 1400s, Stockholm was a center for trade. All goods that went in and out of Sweden passed through its port.

City within a city

Today, Stockholm is an important center for business, politics, and culture. The heart of Stockholm, called Gamla Stan, or Old Town, is very different from the rest of the modern city. Gamla Stan grew from the original settlement on Stadsholmen to include two smaller islands, Riddarholmen and Helgeandsholmen. Castles and centuries-old buildings with arched doorways still stand on Stadsholmen's streets, and people still pray in the Storkyrkan Cathedral, built in the 1100s.

Small shops and cafés line the narrow cobblestone streets of Gamla Stan.

Stockholm, on the eastern coast, Göteborg, on the western coast, and Malmö, in the south, are Sweden's largest cities. They are home to 85 percent of the population. Fortresses once used to guard busy ports, castles that were home to powerful kings and queens, and homes built more than 500 years ago line the cities' harbors and streets. These older buildings stand beside modern skyscrapers, factories, apartment complexes, and maze-like shopping centers.

(top) Stockholm stretches over fourteen islands and part of the mainland. The city is connected by waterways and bridges, like Venice, in Italy. For that reason, Stockholm is nicknamed "Venice of the North." People get around the city by boat, car, bus, or on Tunnelbanan, a subway system that runs above and below the ground.

Other islands

On Riddarholmen, or Knight's Island, there are no shops, no restaurants, and very few homes. Swedes have used the island for more than 700 years as a graveyard for members of the royal family. Helgeandsholmen, or Holy Spirit Island, is home to the Riksdag, or Swedish Parliament, where important political decisions are made. Djurgården is mostly parkland, with museums, an amusement park, and cafés and restaurants.

City of museums

Stockholm is famous for its more than 80 museums. The Skansen Open-Air Museum has more than 150 historic buildings, such as farmhouses, windmills, barns, and churches from all over Sweden, on display. The Vasa Museum houses an entire warship from 1628 that sank to the bottom of Stockholm's harbor the day it set sail.

The Riksdag, or Swedish Parliament, towers over the North Bridge on Helgeandsholmen. It was constructed between 1898 and 1904.

The warship on display at the Vasa Museum was restored in 1961 after it spent 333 years underwater.

Sweden's other cities

Göteborg, Sweden's second-largest city, is sometimes called "the Gateway to the North." This is because more than 11,000 ships, many from southern Europe, pass through its port each year carrying cargo to the rest of Sweden. Fishing is an important industry in Göteborg, and many Gothenburgers eat fresh fish caught in the Skagerrak and Kattegat Seas off the city's coasts.

Malmö's Rådhuset, or city hall, was built in the 1500s. The building has changed several times, and the construction that appears today dates from the 1800s.

Industrial Malmö

Malmö was once named Malmhaug, which means "sandpile" in Swedish, because of the sandy beaches that line its shores. When Malmö was founded in the 1200s, it belonged to Denmark. By the 1400s, the city had grown because of the herring trade, which attracted **merchants** from countries such as Germany who wanted to **export** the fish. They called the city Ellenbogen, which means "elbow" in German, because of the elbow-like curve of its coastline.

Malmö joined Sweden in 1658. By the mid 1800s, the city had grown into a center for industry and transportation. Today, parts for ships, processed food, and textiles produced in Malmö are shipped out of the city's busy ports. Factories, warehouses, and historic buildings, such as Malmöhus, a castle built in the 1500s, still stand along the harbor.

Fishers in Göteborg sell their daily catch at an indoor market called the Fiskhallen. It is nicknamed Feskekörka, or "the Fish Church," because the building's roof and arched windows look like those of a church.

Ancient Visby

Visby, the lone city on Gotland Island, is like a large museum. Visby began as a Viking settlement, and grew into a German merchant town in the 1200s and 1300s. **Medieval** ruins and buildings — from churches to warehouses — stand on almost every street corner amid low wooden and stone houses. A limestone ring wall built to keep out **invaders** stretches nearly two miles (four kilometers) around the city. During *medeltidsveckan*, or Medieval Week, the people of Visby celebrate their historic roots. They dress up as knights, kings, or queens, and attend banquets and jousts, which were tournaments held between knights.

Historic Uppsala

Uppsala, on the banks of the Fyris River in the southwest, was originally a Viking settlement. In 1164, it was made the home of Sweden's archbishop, one of the leaders of the **Roman Catholic Church**. The Uppsala Cathedral took nearly 150 years to build. Across from the cathedral is the Gustavianum, once a palace for the archbishop. Today, it houses the Victoria Museum, where visitors can study ancient Egyptian artifacts, such as statues, pottery, and sarcophagi, which are brightly painted coffins for **mummies**.

In 1995, Visby was named a World Heritage Site by the United Nations Educational, Scientific, and Cultural Organization (UNESCO). UNESCO protects and preserves ancient buildings and monuments, such as this stretch of limestone wall that surrounds the older part of Visby.

From land and sea

Sweden's abundant crops, hearty **livestock**, and catches of fresh fish are mostly sold in grocery stores and local markets within the country. Some large farms plant and harvest hundreds of acres, or hectares of crops, but most farms are smaller and owned by families. Many family-run farms have joined cooperatives. Farmers in cooperatives share equipment and the cost of seeds, and help each other plant and harvest their crops.

Growing crops

The bulk of Sweden's farmland is in the south, but there are pockets of **arable** land all the way up to the Arctic Circle. In the far north, farmers grow crops such as hay and potatoes. In the south, sugar beets, apples, pears, plums, and berries are grown. In the central and southern parts of the country, farmers also grow wheat, barley, and oats.

Raising livestock

More farmers in Sweden raise livestock than grow cash crops. Pigs and chickens are mainly raised in the south. Black-and-white dairy cows, called Holstein cattle, graze in southern pastures. They are raised for their milk. Swedish Red-and-White cattle feed on northern farms. They are used for their milk and meat.

The Sami herd reindeer in the north. Under Swedish law, only the Sami have the right to herd reindeer because it is part of their **heritage**. They also have the right to use other people's land to feed and protect their herds while they are **migrating**.

From seas and lakes

Herring makes up about two-thirds of the fish caught in Sweden. Sweden's fishers catch the silvery fish in the Baltic and North Seas. In the Baltic Sea, they also net pike, perch, and strömming, or Baltic herring. In the saltier North Sea, fishers catch mackerel, cod, and sometimes even shark. A wide variety of fish, such as salmon and trout, also swim in the country's lakes and rivers.

Fishers examine their catch from the Baltic Sea. In the winter, Swedes go ice fishing in lakes high in the mountains, where they catch fish such as Arctic char.

A Sami reindeer herder leads a white reindeer. White reindeer are so rare that the Sami once viewed them as sacred, or special, animals.

A farmer tosses hay on Orust Island, off the western coast. Many farms in Sweden are organic, which means that they do not use chemicals to fertilize their crops or kill insects.

Advanced industries

Sweden's industries are some of the most advanced in the world, partly because the govenment funds research to develop new technologies. Companies manufacture cars, **telecommunications** equipment, power plant equipment, and medicines. These products are sold to Germany, the United Kingdom, the United States, Norway, Finland, and Denmark.

Lumber, pulp, and paper

In forests and on farms, large machines cut down trees. The logs are transported by train or truck to sawmills and pulp and paper factories on the country's eastern and southern coasts. About half the logs are used to make homes and furniture, and the other half are used to make paper. Although there is a high demand for lumber, Sweden's government has taken steps to preserve the country's forests. Sweden practices sustainable logging, which means that farmers have to plant new trees to replace those they cut down.

Plentiful mines

Sweden has mined its underground deposits of iron ore, copper, lead, zinc, silver, and gold for hundreds of years. The most plentiful mineral is iron ore, which was first mined in the 1200s, although archaeologists have found tools made from iron ore that date back to 400 B.C. Today, iron ore is mined mainly in the far north, near the towns of Malmberget and Kiruna. Kiruna has the largest iron ore mine in the world, part of which is under a lake. Copper, lead, zinc, silver, and gold are mined in northern and central Sweden.

(above) Slagheaps pile up at an iron mine outside Kiruna. Slag is waste left over after iron is extracted from rocks. Later, miners use the slag to fill in holes created by mining.

(left) The Swedish government offers money to farmers who convert part of their farmland to timberland. Three-quarters of the country's farms are partially used to grow trees for logging.

Engineering

The iron ore mined in Sweden is mainly used to make steel for farm equipment, trains, aircraft, trucks, ships, and cars. Auto makers Volvo and Saab both began in Sweden. In 1927, businessman Assar Gabrielsson and engineer Gustaf Larson rolled out the first Volvo car. Volvos soon became known for their durability, quality, and safety. Saab unveiled its first car in 1945. The handmade model was the first car to have front-wheel drive, which means that the engine power is sent to the front wheels instead of to the rear wheels.

Since the 1990s, Volvo Cars has been owned by Ford Motor Company, and Saab Automobiles has been part of General Motors, both American companies. The cars' parent, or original, companies are still important in Sweden. The Volvo Group makes buses, trucks, airplane engines, and construction equipment, while The Saab Group makes equipment for defense, **aviation**, and space.

(top) A mechanic assembles parts for a Volvo car at a plant in Göteborg.

Workers sew fabric in an IKEA factory. IKEA was founded in Sweden in 1943. The company designs and sells items for the home, including furniture, lighting fixtures, dishes, and toys. Its furniture comes in pre-made sections that customers put together themselves to save money.

Computers and telephones

Swedes are some of the world's top users of cell phones, computers, and wireless technology, such as wireless headsets that connect people to the Internet. Many of the products they use are made by telecommunications and information technology companies in Sweden. In fact, the Swedish company Ericsson, which makes cell phones, is the second-largest telecommunications company in the world.

Pharmaceuticals and biotechnology

Pharmaceuticals and biotechnology are two of Sweden's fastest growing industries. Pharmaceutical companies make medicines. Scientists in biotechnology companies use small living organisms, such as cells, to make food, medicines, chemicals, and other materials that are useful to people.

A technician assembles a cell phone in an Ericsson plant. More than 80 percent of Swedes own cell phones.

Visitors prepare to go to sleep in their room in the Ice Hotel. The tables, chairs, and even the bed are carved from blocks of ice. Furs and sleeping bags help keep visitors warm.

A visit to Sweden

Sweden's wilderness, royal castles, ancient churches, and Viking ruins draw tens of thousands of tourists to Sweden each year. One of the country's most interesting sites is the Ice Hotel, 100 miles (160 kilometers) north of the Arctic Circle in the Sami town of Jukkasjärvi. The entire hotel is made of snow and ice. The Sami mold snow into beds, tables, chairs, drinking glasses, and even a chandelier. Temperatures inside the hotel hover at a chilly 20° Fahrenheit (–6° Celsius) to keep everything inside frozen. Every spring, the hotel melts, and every winter, the Sami build the hotel again.

Energy

More than 50 percent of Sweden's homes and factories are powered by hydroelectricity. Hydroelectricity is water from lakes and rivers that is dammed and used to create power. The rest of the country's electricity and heat comes from oil and coal **imported** from other countries, and from nuclear power. Nuclear power is generated in reactors, or power stations, that use a type of metal, called uranium, to create energy.

Many people in Sweden do not want the country to use nuclear power because it can be dangerous. In 1986, a nuclear reactor in Chernobyl, Ukraine, exploded. Poisonous waste from the reactor was spread by wind for thousands of miles. Animals and people became sick or died. Even the **lichen** that reindeer in Sweden ate was polluted. After this disaster, the Swedish government began to consider other ways to power the country. These include burning biofuels, which are materials made from Sweden's natural resources, such as peat, branches from felled trees, recycled paper, and pulp waste.

The Swedish government is experimenting with new ways to power the country, such as using windmills, which do not cause pollution.

25

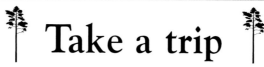 Take a trip

Whether Swedes zoom along superhighways, catch a bus, train, or subway, or hop on a ferry to go to an island, it is easy for them to travel around their country. Sweden has one of the most developed transportation networks in the world.

Safety first

Most Swedish families own at least one car. The three-point seatbelt that motorists use today, which has a shoulder strap attached to a lap belt, was invented by a Swede, Nils Bohlin. It was first installed in Volvo cars in 1959 and is one of the most important traffic safety inventions ever made. Today, seatbelts save one life every six minutes.

On rails

Trains chug along 6,102 miles (9,821 kilometers) of tracks that crisscross Sweden, connecting major cities and towns. The Swedish State Railways run from the northern town of Björkliden, on the Norwegian border, to Trelleborg, on the country's southern tip. The Inlandsbanan, or The Inland Railway, was built in the early 1900s. Inlandsbanan was built to transport iron ore to southern markets and ports. Railway cars still carry freight and tourists along the 800-mile (1,300-kilometer) track that travels from Kristinehamn, a city in the south, to Gällivare, a town north of the Arctic Circle.

(top) Few roads run through Sweden's far north because not many people live there and because snow covers the ground for much of the year, making driving difficult. In the winter, many northerners travel by snowmobile instead of by car. In the summer, they use cars, trucks, or motorcycles, which easily cross the rough terrain.

On water and land

Since the time of the Vikings, who crossed the ocean in sturdy **longships**, Swedes have depended on water travel. Before trains and cars were invented, most Swedes traveled in the summer by canoe, rowboat, ferry, or large ship. In winter, when waterways were frozen, people traveled by foot, ski, snowshoe, or on horseback. Paved roads and railways were built in the 1900s, and replaced waterways as the main mode of transport.

Connecting the countries

Until the year 2000, people traveling from Sweden to Denmark took an hour-long ferry ride across the Öresund Strait. Today, their journey lasts only ten minutes using the Öresund Link. The Öresund Link is made up of an underwater tunnel, road, and bridge on which cars, trucks, buses, and trains travel.

Icebreakers, which are large, heavy ships with pointed fronts, are used in the winter to break the ice in the frozen Baltic Sea so other boats can enter Stockholm's port.

Cyclists race across the five-mile- (eight-kilometer-) long Öresund Bridge. The bridge makes up part of the Öresund Link that connects the Danish capital of Copenhagen with Malmö, in southern Sweden.

Wildlife in the north and south

Fly Agaric mushrooms are beautiful to look at, but unsafe to eat. These mushrooms are so poisonous that people once left bowls of them outside to kill flies.

Sweden is home to a large variety of wildlife. Swedish natural scientist Carolus Linnaeus (1707–1778) studied many of the country's plants and animals from the time he was a young boy. He developed a system for naming and classifying them that is still used around the world today.

Plant life in the forests

Sweden's forests are thick with trees, plants, and bushes that bear raspberries, blueberries, lingonberries, and cloudberries. Many types of mushrooms also sprout on the damp forest floor. Rockroses, lilies of the valley, and other wild flowers bloom in meadows in central and southern Sweden, and orchids grow on the island of Gotland. The delicate lady's slipper is a yellow orchid with blooms that look like tiny shoes.

Everyman's right

Everyone in Sweden has the right to hike, picnic, camp, ski, cycle, swim, and boat in forests and lakes on public and private lands. Swedes call this right *allemansrätten*, or "everyman's right." People are also allowed to pick berries, mushrooms, and wildflowers, except those protected by law, even if they are on someone else's property. The people of Sweden appreciate this right and are careful not to damage the environment by overpicking, littering, or trampling on people's gardens.

In the air

Thousands of migrating birds flock to Sweden's coasts every year, including long-necked cranes, which have stilt-like legs, and sea eagles, which use their rough toes to catch slippery fish to eat. Some birds, such as the brownish-red ptarmigan, stay in Sweden all year. In the winter, these birds sleep in burrows they dig in the snow.

The great gray owl lives in Sweden's forests where it preys on insects, birds, rodents, and hares. It is one of the largest owls in the world, with a wingspan that reaches more than 2 feet (0.6 meters).

Musk oxen have a shaggy, dark brown coat, long, curved horns, and large hoofs that allow them to easily walk on snow. Musk oxen are protected by the government because they are endangered.

Sweden's mammals

Hares, rabbits, badgers, hedgehogs, and red squirrels hop and scurry through Sweden's thick forests. Moose and roe deer are also common. Sweden has several animal species, such as wolves, bears, wolverines, arctic foxes, and lynxes, that are **endangered**. The government has passed laws that make it illegal to hunt, trap, or harm these animals.

Foxes

Red foxes have a rusty red coat with black ears and feet, and a white-tipped tail and snout. They live in mountains, forests, farmland, cellars, sewers, and even city garden sheds. They eat almost anything, including small deer, rabbits, mice, beetles, grasshoppers, earthworms, blackberries, apples, bird food, and even scraps of garbage. Red foxes are considered pests because they root through people's trash and eat small livestock. Many Swedes put up fences or use traps to keep the foxes away.

"King of the Forest"

Swedes call the moose "the King of the Forest." Moose are the largest members of the deer family. They have enormous antlers and long skinny legs that allow them to walk through deep snow. Sweden has more moose than any other country in the world. There are so many moose that they are a traffic hazard! Fences keep moose off most sections of the highway. In areas where the moose cross the highway, signs warn drivers of the danger.

The adult male moose weighs up to 500 pounds (227 kilograms).

Roaming reindeer

The Sami have tamed many of Sweden's reindeer, but wild reindeer still roam free in the northern mountains and forests. These members of the deer family are related to North American caribou. Like caribou, reindeer have adapted to the Arctic climate. They have wide hoofs to help them walk on snow and ice and they use their front hoofs, which are even wider than their back ones, to dig through snow to find plants and lichen to eat. In the spring, male reindeer shed their antlers, which the Sami collect and use for crafts.

Land of lemmings

Mountain lemmings, which look like pudgy mice, live in tunnels they dig in Sweden's north. Lemmings are brown, but change to white in the winter to blend in with their surroundings. According to an old myth, lemmings fling themselves over cliffs and drown themselves in the water below. In reality, lemmings are traveling to a new feeding ground when they run out of food. On their way, they often have to swim across lakes. If strong winds blow and the waters become rough, the lemmings drown.

Herds of reindeer migrate from the north beginning in September, when the weather turns colder and their pasturelands freeze over.

Lemmings hide in underground tunnels from predators such as owls, hawks, and foxes.

Protecting seals

Gray seals live in the Baltic Sea. Their thin bodies allow them to slice through the water with little effort. A layer of thick blubber beneath their skin helps keep them warm in the sea's icy waters. Unfortunately, blubber cannot protect them from harmful pollutants in the water. The pollution has killed thousands of seals in Sweden. In the 1970s, the number of seals plummeted to 2,500. In 1980, a breeding program was established to help the seals survive. That, together with a decrease in pollutants, has helped increase the gray seal population to more than 12,000.

Gray seals eat many kinds of fish, crabs, and other sea creatures. When they have had enough to eat, they haul themselves onto land using their flippers and lie out in the sun.

The environment

Like all countries, Sweden faces environmental problems. Acid rain, which is rain laced with sulfur dioxide, nitrogen oxide, and other harmful chemicals, damages soil and buildings, pollutes lakes and rivers, kills forests, and seriously harms wildlife. The toxic rain forms when smoke from coal and oil burned for power and exhaust fumes from vehicles are released into the air. Swedes first noticed the effects of acid rain in the 1960s, when large numbers of dead fish surfaced in the western lakes. Since then, the country has reduced the amount of coal and oil it uses. Sweden also has laws that restrict cars that pollute too much from being on the roads.

Killer whales swim in family groups called pods in the North Sea, off Sweden's eastern coast. The dorsal fin, on a killer whale's back, can grow to be 6 feet (1.3 meters) long.

Glossary

ancestor A person from whom one is descended

arable Suitable for growing crops

archaeological Related to the study of buildings and artifacts from the past

aviation Aircraft manufacturing and operation

blacksmith A person who makes things from iron

current The flow of water along a certain path in the ocean

endangered In danger of extinction

equator An imaginary line around the middle of the earth that divides the planet into the Northern and Southern Hemispheres

export To sell goods to another country

fertile Able to produce abundant crops or vegetation

fertilize To add soil materials that help plants grow

glacier A very large, slow-moving chunk of ice

heritage Customs, objects, and achievements handed down from earlier generations

homeland A country that is identified with a particular people or ethnic group

import To buy goods from another country

invader A person who enters using force

Latin The language of the ancient Romans

lichen A plant that grows on rocks, trees, or on the ground

limestone A soft rock used for building

livestock Farm animals

longship A long, narrow ship used by the Vikings

medieval Belonging to the period of history from about 500 A.D. to 1500 A.D.

merchant A person who buys and sells goods

migrate To move seasonally from one region to another

mummy A dead body preserved from decay by a method developed by the ancient Egyptians

pharmaceutical Relating to the industry that produces medicines

pulp A mixture of materials, such as wood and fabric, used to make paper products

Roman Catholic Church The Christian Church led by the pope in Rome

telecommunication The science and technology of sending electronic messages by telephone, computer, radio, or television

World War II A war fought by countries around the world from 1939 to 1945

Index